Gorillas

Written by
Pamela McDowell

www.av2books.com

AV² provides enriched content that supplements and complements this book. Weigl's AV² books strive to create inspired learning and engage young minds in a total learning experience.

Your AV² Media Enhanced books come alive with...

Audio
Listen to sections of the book read aloud.

Key Words
Study vocabulary, and complete a matching word activity.

Video
Watch informative video clips.

Quizzes
Test your knowledge.

Embedded Weblinks
Gain additional information for research.

Slide Show
View images and captions, and prepare a presentation.

Try This!
Complete activities and hands-on experiments.

... and much, much more!

Go to **www.av2books.com**, and enter this book's unique code.

BOOK CODE

J396878

AV² by Weigl brings you media enhanced books that support active learning.

Published by AV² by Weigl
350 5th Avenue, 59th Floor
New York, NY 10118
Websites: www.av2books.com   www.weigl.com

Library of Congress Cataloging-in-Publication Data

McDowell, Pamela.
Gorillas / Pamela McDowell.
     pages cm. -- (Amazing primates)
 Includes index.
ISBN 978-1-4896-2878-7 (hardcover : alk. paper) -- ISBN 978-1-4896-2879-4 (softcover : alk. paper) --
ISBN 978-1-4896-2880-0 (single user ebk.) -- ISBN 978-1-4896-2881-7 (multi user ebk.)
1. Gorillas--Juvenile literature. I. Title.
 QL737.P94M39 2014
 599.884--dc23
                                                    2014038983

Printed in the United States of America in Brainerd, Minnesota
1 2 3 4 5 6 7 8 9 0 18 17 16 15 14

122014
WEP081214

Project Coordinator: Katie Gillespie
Art Director: Terry Paulhus

Photo Credits
Weigl acknowledges Getty Images, iStock, Minden Pictures, and Alamy as its primary photo suppliers for this title.

Contents

Meet the
Gorilla

Gorillas are **mammals** that belong to the **primate order**. The gorilla is the largest of the apes. They live only in the forests of Africa. Gorillas rely on the plants in their **habitat** to provide food and shelter. Unlike most other primates, gorillas do not live in trees.

In folklore, gorillas are often made out to be scary and dangerous. In fact, gorillas are not aggressive, but are actually shy, quiet animals. However, the **dominant** male, called a silverback, will defend his troop, if necessary. He may beat his chest, slap the ground, and even roar to scare away a threat.

Gorillas live in groups
called troops. They
include one to four
silverbacks, with females
and their young.

All About Gorillas

There are about 300 living **species** of primates. Gorillas belong to a family of primates called *hominidae*. They are often referred to as greater apes. Like humans, gorillas have large brains compared to their body size. This provides gorillas with good memory and problem-solving skills. In captivity, gorillas have been taught **sign language**.

The largest population of gorillas is the western lowland gorilla, which is found in the forests of West Africa. Western lowland gorillas are smaller and have shorter, lighter hair than mountain gorillas. In 2008, scientists discovered a new group of about 100,000 western lowland gorillas in the Republic of Congo.

Western lowland gorillas are the most common type of gorilla found in zoos.

Comparing Primates

Because there are so many species of primates, scientists split them into subgroups. Each of these subgroups is called a superfamily. There are six superfamilies of primates. Grouping primates makes it easier to study their similarities and differences.

Lemurs

+ **Length:**
3.5 to 28 inches
(9 to 71.1 centimeters)
excluding tail
+ **Weight:**
1.1 ounces to 21
pounds (30 grams
to 9.5 kilograms)
+ **Special Feature:**
Lemurs are the primate
at the highest risk
of **extinction**.

Tarsiers

+ **Length:**
3.6 to 6.4 inches
(9.1 to 16.2 cm)
excluding tail
+ **Weight:**
2.8 to 5.8 ounces
(79.3 to 164.4 g)
+ **Special Feature:**
Tarsiers have
the largest eyes,
compared to body
size, of all mammals.

Lorises

+ **Length:**
7.5 to 15 inches
(19 to 38 cm)
+ **Weight:**
9 ounces to 4.6 pounds
(255 g to 2 kg)
+ **Special Feature:**
Lorises are the only
poisonous primate.
They secrete a **toxic**
oil from a gland in
their elbow.

Old World Monkeys

+ **Length:**
13.4 to 37 inches
(34 to 94 cm)
excluding tail
+ **Weight:**
25 ounces to
110 pounds
(700 g to 50 kg)
+ **Special Feature:**
They have nostrils
that are narrow and
point downward.

New World Monkeys

+ **Length:**
5.5 to 28 inches
(14 to 70 cm)
excluding tail
+ **Weight:**
4.2 ounces to
33 pounds
(120 g to 15 kg)
+ **Special Feature:**
They have nostrils
that are broad
and point outward.

Apes

+ **Length:**
3 to 6 feet
(90 cm to 1.8 meters)
+ **Weight:**
12 to 399 pounds
(5 to 181 kg)
+ **Special Feature:**
Apes do not have tails.
They are the most
intelligent of
all primates.

Gorilla History

Africa
ATLANTIC OCEAN
INDIAN OCEAN

The earliest ancestors of the gorilla lived in Africa more than 25 million years ago. They spread through Asia and Europe. Over time, more than 15 different kinds of apes developed. They lived in places such as Italy and Greece. Apes also developed broader chests, better vision, and larger brains than monkeys.

Close ancestors of today's gorilla developed between 7 and 17 million years ago. They thrived in Africa, near the **equator**. The two species known today, the eastern and western gorilla, emerged about 2 million years ago. Scientists have now defined four subspecies that live in separate areas of Africa.

Humans have had a significant impact on gorilla populations. Since 2000, habitat loss and hunting have increased. Some subspecies of gorillas are now near extinction.

MYSTERY APE

Gorillas were unknown outside Africa until an American missionary described them for the first time, in 1847.

Western lowland gorillas are the smallest of the four subspecies of gorilla.

Where Gorillas Live

Gorillas can be found in the eastern and western parts of Central Africa, close to the equator. The two gorilla species are separated by the Congo Basin. Western gorillas live in lowland and swamp areas. Eastern gorillas live in mountainous areas. Mountain gorillas live in tropical **rainforests** high up in the Virunga mountains.

The troop always moves within its home range of up to 16 square miles (40 sq km). It only travels about 0.5 miles (0.8 km) a day. The silverback decides where the troop will go for food and where they will sleep each night. At dusk, each gorilla builds its own sleeping **nest** from branches and leaves.

Mountain gorillas have thick fur to keep them warm when temperatures fall below freezing.

Gorilla Features

Gorillas will climb trees to pick fruit, and occasionally, to make nests. However, they spend most of their time on the ground. Sometimes, gorillas will stand erect on two feet, but usually they walk on all fours. They have special **adaptations** for surviving on the ground. Powerful arms and a thick, strong chest are useful when traveling on the ground, rather than in the trees.

Getting Closer

1 Coat

- Brownish-gray to black
- Mature males have gray hair on back and head
- Protects from insect bites

2 Face

- Strong jaw to chew tough stems
- 32 teeth
- No hair on the face
- Unique wrinkle pattern on the nose

3 Arms

- Long and muscular
- May be 20 percent longer than legs

4 Hands

- Strong knuckles bear weight when walking
- No hair on hands
- **Opposable** thumb on each hand for grasping food or climbing trees

5 Feet

- Opposable toe on each foot
- Able to walk upright on hind feet

What Do Gorillas Eat?

Gorillas are mainly herbivores, which means that they eat plants. They spend much of their day searching for food on the forest floor. Except for infants, all gorillas eat leaves, shoots, and stems of plants. Some will eat fruit, termites, and caterpillars, as well.

Gorillas have to eat large quantities because the plants they eat are quite low in nutrients. An adult male gorilla may eat more than 40 pounds (18 kg) of food per day. Powerful arms and agile fingers help gorillas find the parts of food they want. A gorilla can shred an entire banana tree to get at the tender part in the middle of the tree. Gorillas move often so they do not use up all the food in one area.

In nature, gorillas rarely drink water. They get enough water from the lush plants they eat.

FOOD SMART

Gorillas eat many different plants, but only certain parts of each one. They know exactly which part of each plant makes the best food.

Gorilla
Life Cycle

Gorillas mate and give birth at any time of the year. Female gorillas are mature at about 10 years old. Male gorillas are ready to mate when they are 12 to 15 years old. Only the dominant male silverback will mate with the females in his troop.

Birth to 3 Months

Newborns weigh about 4.5 pounds (2 kg) and are completely helpless. At first, infants are carried in their mother's arms. Soon, they are able to grip their mother's fur with their hands and feet. They begin crawling at nine weeks old. Infants drink only their mother's milk until about two months of age, when they begin eating vegetation.

Female gorillas only give birth about once every four years. Infant gorillas are born about eight and a half months after mating. Twins are very rare for gorillas. Both females and males are patient, gentle, and protective of their young. The mother takes cares of the young gorilla for three to four years.

10 Years and Older

Female gorillas usually stay with the troop until they are ready to mate. Then, they move to another troop or to a lone male. Young males may leave to start a troop of their own. If they stay, they will not become dominant unless the silverback dies. In nature, gorillas live about 35 years.

3 Months to 10 Years

Baby gorillas begin to walk at about six months. By 18 months, they can travel short distances. However, for the first three years, they still ride most often on their mother's back and sleep in her nest. They nurse for up to three years. Young male and female gorillas look very similar until they are about eight years old. Then, the males grow taller and heavier.

Conservation of Gorillas

Today, researchers think there are between 100,000 and 200,000 gorillas left in nature. Only 17 percent of these gorillas live in protected areas. Gorillas have no natural **predators**. It is human activities, such as logging, mining, farming, and war that have destroyed their habitat. Deadly diseases and hunting also threaten the gorilla population.

Eastern gorillas are now listed as **endangered**. There are even fewer western gorillas left in the world. They are considered to be **critically endangered**. However, education and **ecotourism** are helping people focus on gorilla conservation. Eight African countries have made laws against capturing and hunting gorillas. Many conservation groups are working hard to protect gorillas and their habitat.

HELPING OUT

Dian Fossey was an American scientist who did much to educate the world about gorillas.

Some centers care for orphaned gorillas. Once the gorillas are old enough to take care of themselves, they are released.

Myths and Legends

Many of the **indigenous** people of Africa have strong feelings about gorillas. They may fear, hate, or **worship** gorillas. In many groups, animals such as gorillas, leopards, and orangutans are chosen as a family **totem**. In such groups, it is **taboo** to hunt a gorilla, as it is believed this will cause the totem owner to die.

In some villages, people practice traditional medicine. Here, gorilla parts, such as the skull, bones, heart, and hair, are used to treat illnesses. Some groups believe that medicine men can transform into gorillas to climb into the treetops to harvest leaves.

Gorillas will test if branches are strong enough to support their weight before climbing on them.

Opposable Thumb Experiment

Like other great apes, gorillas have opposable thumbs. This means the thumbs can move in many directions, and touch the palm of the hand and each finger. Gorillas use their opposable thumbs to grasp plant stems, pick up termites, and break fruit apart. Infants use them to grip their mother's fur. Humans also use their opposable thumbs to do many things each day. Try this experiment to test the usefulness of your opposable thumbs.

Materials Needed: tape, a piece of paper, a pencil, safety scissors, a few coins

STEP 1 Try each of these activities:

- Write your name on the piece of paper with the pencil.

- Untie your shoe, take it off, and toss it to a friend.

- Put your shoe back on and retie it.

- Draw a large circle on the paper and cut it out with the safety scissors.

- Drop the coins on the floor and pick them up.

STEP 2 Have someone help you tape your thumbs to the first finger of each hand.

STEP 3 Now, try each of the activities again. Which of the activities are more difficult? Are any of them impossible to do without using your thumbs?

STEP 4 Gorillas also have an opposable toe on each foot. What things could you do if you had opposable toes? Write a paragraph describing how opposable toes could be useful.

5 Know Your FACTS

Test your knowledge of gorillas.

1 What might a silverback do to defend his troop?

2 What are the main differences between apes and monkeys?

3 What food do all gorillas, except infants, eat?

4 How long will a mother gorilla care for her young?

5 What human activities affect gorilla populations?

ANSWERS

1. Beat his chest, roar, slap the ground

2. Apes have broader chests, better vision, and larger brains

3. Leaves, shoots, and stems of plants

4. Three to four years

5. Hunting, logging, mining, agriculture, diseases, and war

Key Words

adaptations: adjustments to the natural environment

critically endangered: at the very highest risk of no longer living any place on Earth

dominant: stronger and more powerful than another animal

ecotourism: travel to areas that conserve the environment

endangered: at serious risk of no longer living any place on Earth

equator: the imaginary line around the middle of Earth dividing it into northern and southern hemispheres

extinction: no longer living any place on Earth

habitat: the environment in which an animal lives

indigenous: the first or original people, animals, or plants of a place

mammals: warm-blooded live-born animals that drink milk from their mother

nest: a structure an animal makes out of branches and twigs for sleeping

opposable: able to touch the other fingers of the same hand or other toes of the same foot

order: in biology, a level of classification

poisonous: able to produce a harmful substance to protect itself from prey

predators: animals that hunt other animals

primate: a mammal with a relatively large brain, flexible hands and feet, and good eyesight

rainforests: dense forests with heavy rainfall

sign language: a communication system that uses visual gestures, such as manual, facial, and other body movements

species: animals that share many features and can produce offspring together

taboo: something banned or forbidden

totem: an animal or natural object that a family or clan values as a symbol of ancestry

toxic: harmful substance produced by an animal or plant

worship: to show reverence for

Index

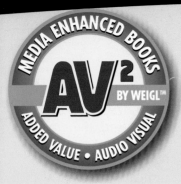

Log on to www.av2books.com

AV[2] by Weigl brings you media enhanced books that support active learning. Go to www.av2books.com, and enter the special code found on page 2 of this book. You will gain access to enriched and enhanced content that supplements and complements this book. Content includes video, audio, weblinks, quizzes, a slide show, and activities.

AV[2] Online Navigation

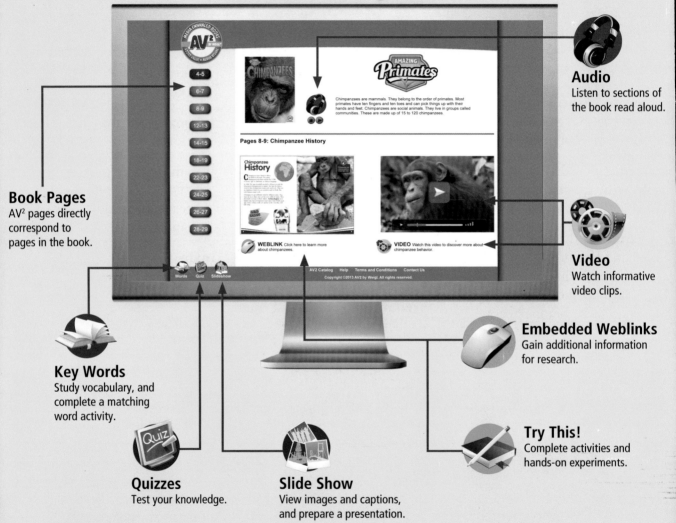

Audio
Listen to sections of the book read aloud.

Book Pages
AV[2] pages directly correspond to pages in the book.

Video
Watch informative video clips.

Key Words
Study vocabulary, and complete a matching word activity.

Embedded Weblinks
Gain additional information for research.

Try This!
Complete activities and hands-on experiments.

Quizzes
Test your knowledge.

Slide Show
View images and captions, and prepare a presentation.

AV[2] was built to bridge the gap between print and digital. We encourage you to tell us what you like and what you want to see in the future.

Sign up to be an AV[2] Ambassador at www.av2books.com/ambassador.

Due to the dynamic nature of the Internet, some of the URLs and activities provided as part of AV[2] by Weigl may have changed or ceased to exist. AV[2] by Weigl accepts no responsibility for any such changes. All media enhanced books are regularly monitored to update addresses and sites in a timely manner. Contact AV[2] by Weigl at 1-866-649-3445 or av2books@weigl.com with any questions, comments, or feedback.